W9-BFW-941

The Translation of Babel

The Translation of Babel

Poems by Scott Cairns

The University of Georgia Press
Athens and London

© 1990 by Scott Cairns
Published by the University of Georgia Press
Athens, Georgia 30602
All rights reserved
Designed by Betty P. McDaniel
Set in Galliard
The paper in this book meets the guidelines for
permanence and durability of the Committee on
Production Guidelines for Book Longevity of the
Council on Library Resources.

Printed in the United States of America

94 93 92 91 90   5 4 3 2 1

Library of Congress Cataloging in Publication Data

Cairns, Scott.
    The translation of babel : poems / by Scott Cairns.
        p.   cm.
    ISBN 0-8203-1199-5 (alk. paper). —
    ISBN 0-8203-1200-2 (pbk. : alk. paper)
    I. Title.
PS3553.A3943T73   1990
811'.54—dc20   89-37663
                    CIP

British Library Cataloging in Publication Data available

for my dad

Bud Cairns
(1928–1988)

Acknowledgments

Some of these poems have previously appeared in the following
publications:

The Atlantic Monthly: "Homeland of the Foreign Tongue"
Chariton Review: "You Wreck Your Car," "Imperial Theology,"
"Chore"
College English: "False Angels"
Cottonwood Review: "Lucifer's Epistle to the Fallen"
Denver Quarterly: "Lost Cities: Calvino"
The Great Stream Review: "Our Lost Angels"
The New Republic: "In Praise of Darkness," "Another Song,"
"Still Waiting," "Embalming," "Acts," "The Mummy Viewed"
Quarterly West: "Memory"
Shenandoah: "Leaving Florianopolis"
Tailwind: "Early Frost"
Texas Review: "Archaeology: The First Lecture"
Western Humanities Review: "Invitation to a Wedding,"
appearing as "The Book of Forms"
Zone 3: "Yellow"

Contents

III. *The Translation of Raimundo Luz*

The Translation of Babel

Invitation to a Wedding

Since this is the west, where most borders
approach the quaint artifice
of geometry, so the days themselves achieve
their brief expressions of form.

And likewise, the stuff of days finds some manner
for its gestures: The forms
of greeting, and of play, the sober forms
of worship, the forms love takes

when the mind is rested, the sometimes
astonishing forms of speech.
And then, as in any formal gathering,
the familiar dose of convention—

the cosmetics of the bride and groom,
stiff fabrics to keep the body straight,
flowers to hide the shortfalls of the room,
the wooden orchestrations of our band.

What joy one takes from such square dances
is not so much the familiar steps, more
likely, what lies hidden, or faintly seen—
his false step, her exaggerated spin.

So, as you might accept any public invitation
and chance to overhear the private terms,
you might lift this book from among the others,
this sad and arbitrary book, this book of forms.

I. *Acts*

And how hear we every man
in our own tongue, wherein we were born?

—*Luke, Acts of the Apostles*

Acts

So little to be done and so much time.
I nearly told the giddy crowd outside
the Pentecostal church they might go home
—for all the good they'd do—or spend the evening
with their own queer group there on the lawn
instead of squeezing again into their failing
buses for another dose of humility
at selected crossroads, the worst parts of town.

But I know these types too well. If I had
said a word, the tall boy with those startling ears
and disquieting blue skin would be the one
to bleat some trembling prayer while the others
quivering as if shocked would lay on me
a crown of hands. So I just stood there,
watching their sincere, low-rent theater,
this eager preparation for their war.

Years ago, I was unlucky enough
to find another of these witless boys
shouting at my corner, cataloguing
sin with an astonishing lack of charm.
In time, the crowd abandoned humor, but
they couldn't shut him up. From that grim press,
another boy—some squat lump with rolled sleeves—
approached the believer and slapped him hard.

When the witness didn't move, the hand
came up again. As the third blow barked I found
myself shoving in, hating both of them,
but pulling out the one I hated most

and pulling him to my own door. Away
from the jubilant cattle at the crossing,
my indiscreet relation dropped wholly
down, forsaking all for his appalling tongues.

Memory

The problem with memory is that most
memories are dull; what happens,
in general, is mostly dull. I remember

how dull my own boyhood was, the long wait
for something to happen nearly always
ending in disappointment—Martha Watson's

summer dresses nearly falling away,
but never really falling away.
But suppose one morning without rain she found

her way to my room, the sun entering
with her and lighting up the window
and the bed, lighting her dress as it became

liquid and fell down her arms. I think that
would be interesting. And her sad,
small breasts and her strong thighs, lighted up,

would be interesting. I think I would find
everything about her visit
tremendously interesting. That's why even

a little of this extravagance is
so necessary, why, in the strange
and unlikely light of such visitations,

the actual nearly always pales into
embarrassment. It's too serious
to want around, too earnest to put up with

for very long; its straight face can
turn laughter bitter in your mouth, choke
the best parts of your past, ruin your life.

Early Frost

This morning the world's white face reminds us
that life intends to become serious again.
And the same loud birds that all summer long
annoyed us with their high attitudes and chatter
silently line the gibbet of the fence a little stunned,
chastened enough.

They look as if they're waiting for things
to grow worse, but are watching the house,
as if somewhere in their dim memories
they recall something about this abandoned garden
that could save them.

The neighbor's dog has also learned to wake
without exaggeration. And the neighbor himself
has made it to his car with less noise, starting
the small engine with a kind of reverence. At the window
his wife witnesses this bleak tableau, blinking
her eyes, silent.

I fill the feeders to the top and cart them
to the tree, hurrying back inside
to leave the morning to these ridiculous
birds, who, reminded, find the rough shelters,
bow, and then feed.

Another Song

Most mornings I wake up slowly. That's just
the way I am. I wake up slow as I can, listening first
to one thing, then another. The milk bottles chiming

just outside the door, then the milktruck idling in the street.
If I'm lucky, the girl through the wall will be singing
and I'll hear her next, singing while she dresses. Maybe

she's brushing her hair, or tying the ribbon for her stocking
—that would be nice. And out in the hall, some man will
probably kiss Miss Weitz good-bye again—yes, I believe

those are their lowered voices now, and that is his cough.
Others are coming out now, their doors opening and closing so
variously, too many to sort out. Why sort them out? And now

the factory whistle is telling the night shift that enough is
    enough.
Now I hear myself humming along, joining in this little chorus
of good intentions. When everything is ready, I'll go out.

Yellow

The town is much larger than you recall,
but you can still recognize the poor:
they vote to lose every chance they get, their faces
carry the tattoo of past embarrassments,

they are altogether too careful. This girl,
here in the print dress, pretending to shop
for an extravagance, the too slow way
her hand lingers between the colors along

the rack, her tentative hold on the clasp—
sure signs she knows she has no business here.
Soon enough she'll go home again with nothing
especially new in her hand, but no one

needs to rush things. The afternoon itself
is unhurried, and the lighted air outside
the store has lilacs in it. Her hand finds
a yellow dress. I think she should try it on.

You Wreck Your Car

Maybe you'll live, maybe some fluke will have
the emergency crew waiting with their pants on.

It could be they weren't even sleeping, just
playing cards or eating fried chicken inside

the station house, drinking nothing but, say,
coffee, just two or three blocks from your mistake.

It turns out they had been ready, eager
even, to make tracks to your accident. They

live for this. Odds are you'll be light-headed,
too giddy maybe to notice much about

how their hands dance, altogether, above
your wounds, or how they pamper you to the cot,

flatter you against all that you deserve,
and float you to the hospital. Your eyes may

fail now, and that familiar weariness
will coax you into accepting sleep, so you'll

never know how, even as you gesture
toward death, your angels are most alive.

Imperial Theology

Admit it. The Haida were sons of bitches.
Everyone knew that much. While all the good
tribes minded their own stretches of beach, sifting
tide pools for shellfish, taking turns hauling in
salmon, maybe slapping one another
on the back each time someone had nerve enough
to drag in a whale, the Haida worked
to develop a richer taste, a preference for food
other people labored to produce,
and a taste for the necessary
blood they had to spill to get the food.
Their religion was simple: What is good
for the Haida makes good theology.
Their holy men blessed them, after their fashion,
and gave elaborate thanks to their gods
each time the proud elect harvested
another fishing village with their clubs.

Infirmities

Some mornings, you know you've seen
things like this before.
The kind woman across the street
is lame, and her daughter is lame.

Some defect they've had since birth
is working to dissolve their bones.
The boy three doors down
is blind. And the idiot
girl who sweeps up at the market
insists all day on her own
strange tune. And sometimes they seem
happy enough and sometimes
you might find one alone, muffling
grief with a coat sleeve.

And the shy way the blind boy
laughs when he stumbles
makes you laugh with him some mornings.
Some mornings it hurts to see.

Chore

Of course, what we actually feel is too much
a grab-bag of longing to be anything so simple

as an emotion. What we actually feel could never
be pinned down to a word. My father

was dying, and I was home for a visit.
I did a few chores to help us all get ready.

To speak of how I felt would be a mistake.
I was splitting firewood, loading the woodbox.

It was hard work, and I found some pleasure in it.
I was at the back corner of my father's house,

a place I hadn't seen in years, working easily
and well, my shirt off in the last heat of summer.

Wiping the sweat from my face, I looked up
and saw him, saw that he had been watching me.

We met as well as we could. Behind him a huge jay
bowed a heavy branch. I pointed to the hysterical bird.

Nothing much happened after that. I swung the axe
until I finished the work.

Another Kiss

Far sweeter as a greeting, this parting
of lips became the concluding gesture
love would bear between my father and me.
In this last hour of his death his fever
had retreated so that as my kiss found
the smooth passage of his neck, I felt
how the cold surprise was beginning there.

And so we waited, and I kept my sight
fixed upon his face, which worked with less
conviction—which appeared to acquiesce.
I studied his preference for fainter effort:
the softening of his brow, the rounding
edges and, as if he could speak, the slight
movement of his lips, nearly opening.

All of this, so I would remember the hour
and the moment of my father's death,
so I might rehearse the silent language
of this final speech. His lungs were filling
and gave him less and less reason to breathe.
Lifting briefly, his lips in the semblance
of a kiss, and a kiss, a third kiss, he was gone.

After the Last Words

By now I'm dead. Make what you will of that.
But granted you are alive, you will need
to be making something more as well. Prayers
have been made, for instance, but (trust me)

the dead are oblivious to such sessions.
Settle instead for food, nice meals (thick soup):
invite your friends. Make lively conversation
among steaming bowls, lifting heavy spoons.

If there is bread (there really should be bread),
tear it coarsely and hand each guest his share
for intinction in the soup. Something to say?
Say it now. Let the napkins fall and stay.

Kiss each guest when time comes for leaving.
They may be embarrassed, caught without wit
or custom. (See them shifting from foot to
foot at the open door?) Could be you will

repeat your farewells a time or two more
than seems fit. But had you not embraced them
at such common departures prayers will
fall as dry crumbs, nor will they comfort you.

Embalming

You'll need a corpse, your own or someone else's.
You'll need a certain distance; the less you care
about your corpse the better. Light should be
unforgiving, so as to lend a literal
aspect to your project. Flesh should be putty;
each hair of the brows, each lash, a pencil mark.

If the skeleton is intact, its shape may
suggest beginnings of a structure, though even here
modification might occur; heavier
tools are waiting in the drawer, as well as wire,
varied lengths and thicknesses of doweling.
Odd hollows may be filled with bundled towel.

As for the fluids, arrange them on the cart
in a pleasing manner. I prefer we speak
of *ointments*. This notion of one's annointing
will help distract you from a simpler story
of your handiwork. Those people in the parlor
made requests, remember? Don't be concerned.

Whatever this was to them, it is all yours now.
The clay of your creation lies before you,
invites your hand. Becoming anxious? That's good.
You should be a little anxious. You're ready.
Hold the knife as you would a quill, hardly at all.
See the first line before you cross it, and draw.

The End of the World

The end of the world occurs with the first thaw. Waking from his first restful night in many months—a night without shivering, without cramping muscles—the last man lifts his head from the straw, hears snow-melt trickling, sees morning light through the window's ice, smells the scent of earth, lies back, and dies because he cannot bear to go through it all again.

But that is a very limited view of the event. The end was more than the final exhaustion of the last man. Actually, some of the most interesting events of human history occurred just prior to this last gesture, which is not surprising if you take into account the fact that, in the last years of human experience, irony flourished.

The last man was a Jew, a fact that he ignored for many years—most of his life, really. But as years passed and he came to realize his status as last man, the fact of his Jewishness became an insider's joke. The first time he laughed in his adult life was related to his Jewishness, he was picking rust from a can of peaches when he remembered *Torah,* the covenant.

But, as you might suspect, there were many years when the last man was not alone, was not, in simple words, the last man, not yet. Twenty years before the end of the world, the last man was married to one of the last women; they even had a son together and for several months entertained hopes of survival. Later, they parted, mostly out of bewilderment.

If you must know, the last man thought he was the last man some time before he actually was. Many miles away, the second-to-last man lived quietly in a shopping mall. He cut his foot on something in the hardware store and died of tetanus. All told, there were about two years when the last man was mistaken, but that had no effect upon perceptions concerning his lastness.

The last man was the last for about five years and three months, though you could argue he was last for seven years and three months, depending. Anyway, one of the more curious outcomes was that he forgot his name. There is no reliable method for determining when, exactly, he forgot his name; by the time he realized he had forgotten his name he'd also forgotten when he last knew it.

Even so, it is safe to say that he was without a name for the better part of his last year. This was the beginning of an astonishing freedom. The last man had always enjoyed books; that was fortunate. Following the loss of his name, and having acquiesced to lastness, the last man became the first reader. He shrugged off identity and became multiple, embracing all.

He became the author of many great works, indestructible works. The loss of his name was the beginning of this translation, and the loss of his name brought about the loss of many other limitations. He looked up from his canned peaches, looked around, saw the end of the world, and felt pretty relaxed.

As an agnostic, the last man had seldom prayed. But as his final days diminished, he began to address God. He also began to answer, to respond to his own petitions. As God of the last man, he was compelled to deny every request—the plea for companionship, for understanding, for true wisdom, for a pure heart. He denied the last man everything, but always with good reason.

II. *Leaving Florianopolis*

Soon I shall know who I am.
—*Borges, "In Praise of Darkness"*

In Praise of Darkness

Here, behind this attic door is Borges,
waiting in a straight chair, bound there
by thin wire and by rags. Soon you will
ask him the questions again, and soon

he will say his answers, his insane
and foolish words, smiling as if he had said
enough, as if he had answered what you've asked.
And you will hit him again, and split

his skin; you'll invent pain and slowly
let him know what it is you've made.
But, as before, nothing will have changed.
If he speaks at all he'll only say his

nonsense to the air until you must
hit again to make him stop. So you
come to hate the hand that pulls open
the attic door, that gives you Borges,

waiting in a straight chair, looking out
from the corner of an attic room. There is
a wash of light from the window, and it warms
his face, his arms; he feels it pouring

through the neat, dark suit he wears.
You believe he is mad. He is too old
for this and nearly blind, and the light
on his face makes him beautiful.

When you enter the room, he sees
an angel enter; he turns his head
toward your noise, his face expectant.
You have never been so loved.

Lucifer's Epistle to the Fallen

Lucifer, Son of the Morning, Pretty Boy,
Rose Colored Satan of Your Dreams, Good as Gold,
you know, God of this World, Shadow in the Tree.

Gorgeous like you don't know! Me, Sweet Snake, jeweled
like your momma's throat, her trembling wrist. Tender
as my kiss! Angel of Darkness! Angel

of Light! Listen, you might try telling *me*
your troubles; I promise to do what I can.
Which is plenty. Understand, I can kill

anyone. And if I want, I can pick
a dead man up and make him walk. I can
make him dance. Any dance. Angels don't

get in my way; they know too much.
God, I love theater! But listen, I know
the sorry world He walks you through.

Him! Showboat with the Heavy Thumbs! Pretender
at Creation! Maker of Possibilities!
Please! I know why you keep walking—you're skittish

as sheep, and life isn't easy. Besides,
the truth is bent to keep you dumb to death.
Imagine! The ignorance you're dressed in!

The way you wear it! And His foot tickling
your neck. Don't miss my meaning; I know none
of this is your doing. The game is fixed.

Dishonest, if you ask me. So ask. God
knows how I love you! My Beauty, My Most
Serious Feelings are for you, My Heart turns

upon your happiness, your ultimate
wisdom, the worlds we will share. Me, *Lucifer*.
How can such a word carry fear? *Lucifer,*

like love, like song, a lovely music lifting
to the spinning stars! And you, my cooing
pigeons, my darlings, my tender lambs, come, ask

anything, and it will be added to your
account. Nothing will be beyond us; nothing
dares touch my imagining.

False Angels

If they can remember heaven at all,
the memory is a version you would not
recognize: There was some business
about light, a disturbing radiance
flowing from each stern figure in their past.

Often, they have bad dreams, visitations
of endless movement in limitless space,
a gesture which once might have brought
. . . was it elation? which now evokes mere
queasiness, heart's vertigo. The worst?

An unbearable memory of Him:
that turbulence in which they would swim,
appalling embrace, eternal chasm,
that heady balm, passion's flood and fire,
which without understanding they desire.

Homeland of the Foreign Tongue

Each morning we begin again. My wife
wakes me with a shove, and condescends to try
her sorry Deutsch with me; she's chewing mud.
God, she's dumb. I tell her so, but mostly
in a dialect she never understands.
Carefully now, she mouths her thanks and takes me

by the hand to the dampness of the trough,
where she leaves me throwing water on my face.
I wash those parts I want to wash, begin
my bump along the wall to the sour kitchen,
where coffee waits and something tasteless chills
against the plate. Grace is blind, and probably

deaf as well, happens only where angels
let it—nowhere you'll ever find in time.
I've never seen the woman's face, though once,
too far from here to count for much, I wished I could.
But it's morning come again, and she,
as is her habit, begins to sing above the soup.

Somewhere, some angel pities me, as God
must once have pitied her: Her voice forgets
its tenement, and I neglect the words.

Lost Cities: Calvino

Already, the room seems smaller, and I forget which
version of the world I was visiting last. My eyes
have found a way of closing by themselves, and if I sleep,
I feel as if I could sleep forever in my dream.

For a time, at any rate, the way seemed clear enough.
It was as if, if your town were dying, you still had choices,
as if you could die right along with that unhappy place,
or live as you might, somehow beyond its pettiness.
So, I look at myself and I imagine a man I love
lying too quietly across a pallet, barely breathing,
and losing ground while I watch.

In this version, maybe I don't know him well,
but have only come across some things he's done,
things that have made me better, or have made me
think more generously than I might have on my own.
That would be reason enough to love him, I think.
So today I imagine I love him as I love myself.
I wish him well.

When I was a boy, I stepped off a train and had
a beautiful thought: There are places in the world
where people have been dying forever. For instance,
you step out from your train some bright yellow day in April
and there you have it, there beneath your feet—that silent,
crushed city. It occurs to me that I don't have to settle
for that kind of waste, and so I don't.

Tired as I am, I imagine my city alive again. And if I want,
I make it better than it was, and the people better

than they would have been. If you let it, a lie so generous
as this can redeem the whole embarrassment. It's not
a bad way to travel, bumping into remarkable towns
you might have missed, or maybe mourned for. There is
no unnecessary art to this. Just imagine: From his heaven, God

watches all these poor, dim images approaching the invisible
door, again and again, in fear. Could be he pulls his beard
wanting to wake those shadows up to loveliness, to the joy
in making a new world from nothing, or a world
from nearly nothing, a world from the giddy expectations
crowded in a single word.

Then what of those Lost Cities? Of course they can't be
truly lost, only hidden behind some regrettable veil
of grief, maybe dying for the lack of a little humor
to put some color to their faces once again. Against such
possibilities, death has no significance, or not enough.
I think again of the cricket which woke me late last night,
or which woke me once some night long ago, or perhaps

I only imagine a cricket trying to keep itself awake
by singing the only song it has, but giving everything it has
to—is it loveliness? I like to think there must be some deeply
buried artifact compelling something more than style,
more than postures struck. Hearts, for instance, pronouncing
all they hear or think they hear as clearly as they can.

And now this man I never knew well enough is dying,
and dying sings more than I can hold. My worlds increase
without me. They pull me after them. Me, Calvino.
In my solitary bed I'm not alone. *God love us, Where*
is the lovely book I lent the boy? The boy who had no idea

what it was he held, held weeping for his loneliness and pain.
I couldn't help him, but handed him a book I loved.

Unlike these tormented ones, I cannot live on happenstance.
I am too happy to make a poem from what I know.
Bless me I am deeply tired now. A thousand invisible cities
all demanding my attention. If you love me wish me well.

An Irony

Like looking too long into a father's death,
this puzzling affection can require too much.
Then comes the greater trouble, when you begin
to suspect your words—even those that caress
the tongue—point only to other, ever
diminishing words, or only to desires,
vague and untouched by the welcomed response
of flesh, the deeper assurance of live bone.
Few can bear to suspect how little
their conversations have to do with breath.

Coming Forth

I'm sorry, I have a hard time not laughing
even now. This ridiculous grin

won't get off my face. Dying did it,
though I don't remember much about

being dead. Sometimes, horrible things happen:
children die, famine sets in, whole towns

are slapped down and turned to dust by earthquake.
I can't help it, but these things start me

laughing so I can't stop. My friends all hate me.
The morning my sister cracked her hip,

I was worthless; I had to run clear out
to the clay field to keep anyone from seeing

how it broke me up I know. You think
I'm trash, worse than a murderer

or a petty god. I suppose I am.
I just get this quiver started

in me every time someone I know dies and stays dead.
I tremble all over and have to hold

myself, as if some crazy thing in me
were anxious to get out. I told you

I can't remember being dead. I can't.
But this weakness in my knees, or in my throat

keeps me thinking—whatever comes next
should be a thousand worlds better than this.

The Sheriff's Last Pronouncement

Go out there if you want to; I am,
frankly, too weary of this business

to care. But stick around if you don't
mind hearing the truth. I'll only tell

it once. After that, I'm going back
to my books for a little real life.

Your old friend, that Hood, is nothing but
a pimply kid who pockets every

coin he takes. The lout won't even spend,
just likes to watch the gold pile up.

I'm told he even pees on it just
to keep his sorry band of pissants

from touching any of it. I may as well
tell you now—your sweet Marian

hasn't been a maid since she was eight.
She pees on her gold too. For all I know,

the whole lot of them does nothing but
steal, copulate, and pee. It isn't fear

that keeps me from the forest; the whole
place reeks. Give me Nottingham *any*

day—a man knows what he can touch
and what he can't. Your merry band

can have the whole stinking world and *all*
the gold. I'm not going out again.

Archaeology: The First Lecture

But we needn't be troubled with much more
talk of these, except to say that their gods
were bloody, and so *they* were bloody; they
also stank, ate meat, and left their feces
where they fell. Beyond these things, they remain
for the most part unremarkable, not
generous to further study, and sadly dull.

I recall my own disappointment in
their bones—dark, stiff things, just fists and twisted
limbs; crania—fruitless gourds, uninteresting
as dust. Murder, you'll note, continued to be
their most natural cause of death, though
these murders were themselves uninteresting
—typically something blunt cracking a thick skull.

We may as well move to another locale,
unless some question remains concerning
these thugs, or their demise, or the simple
construction of their weapons, which was their
chief religion, it seems, and their only art.
Where such knowledge leads—who would say?
Surrounding debris suggests their bellies were full.

Leaving Florianopolis

Carlos I said to myself, which was so
unlike me because my name is not Carlos,

but *Carlos,* I said, *Never fail to do
what is necessary under heaven.*

Good advice, I thought at the time
and think so still. But, as necessity

was flourishing so remarkably well
upon departure, I had to lie down.

It was then, opening one eye ever
so slightly, I witnessed the deft flex

of anonymous legs approaching.
These were long and slender and of a hue

a painter in oils would call sienna, use
to limn his garden stalks. I closed my eyes

as she whose dark limbs approached leaned close,
her breath like exotic flowers—all of them blue.

Into the cup of my ear she breathed *Eugene,*
or was it *Raymond,* thinking to wake me

for some device in the hammock. I feigned sleep
and so allowed her whatever game she pleased.

She changed my name many times, but for each
small outrage of the tongue her invention

more than compensated. She wore me so,
I had to feign waking to plead sincere

exhaustion. Listening then to what I took
to be her burnt sienna feet, staccato

across the bright tiles, I dreamed once again
of Florianopolis, that untoward port

whose intriguing flues line the coastal curve
in such alluring designs, and whose women

are forever bidding strangers farewell
with lush gestures, their cool habit of approach,

their lips' blue buds parting, their famous kiss.
Oh, Carlos! How can you leave like this?

Still Waiting

Yes, and after all of this we stand, still waiting
for those quaint people to arrive, and to accomplish
their famous work among us. And isn't it just like
barbarians to make us wait. It's been so long since

we first made ready that the town could use another
coat of paint. Someone should probably feed
the children. The senator might as well take his seat.
The feasting tables have begun to stink; servant boys

can't keep the birds away. Without a breath of wind,
the pennants hang like laundry. The afternoon is
failing altogether. Evening, as they say, is already
at the gate. So I embroider this longest part

of an exaggerated day, drawing with a stick
to relieve the wait. I should have known—I'm sure
I told them—these foreigners are always on their way;
they are forever late. Just the same, we know they must

be coming. What else could they do? They have
so little patience, no interest in boardgames, books,
or conversation. Slow as they are, they could hardly
stay home—so easily bored, so discontent, so great.

The Mummy Viewed

Laid out in delicate repose for visitants
like us, who come dumbly believing we have come
for another of those fifty-cent amusements
and wish we had not come, had left the children home,

there she is: a girl, ancient, perfectly chaste
though stripped of more than clothes, stripped of all
so that even what survives, formally debased,
has suffered an alien and drastic memorial.

And then the puzzlement: given spirit and flesh,
which element has been surrendered, which displaced?
as crowding we peer from ordinary callousness
into the carved Egyptian jasper of her face—

like staring into any neat and bloodless wound
whereof the pain is disproportionate: a paper cut,
those open, emptied hands Christ offered to the room
of Thomases, or this queer human apricot.

Regarding the Monument

But roughly but adequately it can shelter
what is within (which after all
cannot have been intended to be seen).
—ELIZABETH BISHOP

Of course it is made of *would,* and *want,*
the threads and piecework of *desire.* Its shape
is various, always changing but always
insufficient, soliciting revision.

       I thought you said it was made of *wood.*
       You said it was made of wood.

Never mind what I may have said; I might
have said anything to bring you this close
to the monument. As far as that goes,
parts of it *are* wood, parts are less, more.

       Some kind of puzzle? What can it do?
       If the wind lifts again we're in trouble.

Certain of its features endure—its more
sepulchral qualities—whether it gestures
ahead or back, the monument
is always in some sense memorial.

       Is it safe? It looks so unstable.
       Do you think it's safe to come so close?

I don't think it's safe, but I don't think safe matters.
It's changing. Even now. Watch how it turns
into its new form, taking something
of what it was, taking something else.

I don't feel well. Does it have to do that?
Is it growing? Still? Something must be wrong.

The monument is growing still, even if
diminishment must be a frequent stage
of its progress. If we return tomorrow
it may appear much less; it may seem gone.

I don't see the point. What is the point?
I'm leaving now; you stay if you want.

But the part that lies buried, its foundation,
will forge its machinery ever and again,
and the wind will return it to motion,
if more powerfully, and more horribly.

III. *The Translation of Raimundo Luz*

I show you a mystery: we shall not all sleep,
but we shall all be changed.
  —*Paul to the Corinthians*

Biographical Note

Raimundo Luz is the greatest postmodern poet writing in Portuguese. He has never left his birthplace, Florianopolis, Brazil. His father was a mender of fishing nets, his mother a saloon singer. He has no formal education, having gathered all he knows from books. He reads seven modern languages, also ancient Hebrew, ancient Greek, and Latin. Luz is best known as a radical theologian, identifying himself paradoxically as a Christian-Marxist. He is a devoted family man, a fan of American rhythm and blues, an accomplished cook, and a fiction.

The Translation of Raimundo Luz

I. MY INFANCY

How like a child I was! So small and so
willing! And the world was extravagant,

and beyond reach even then. All those lovely
apparitions flitting close, and then away—

I loved them. Even their inconstancy.
God was always tapping his curious

music in my head. I'm sure I *seemed* aloof,
but the opposite was true—such a pleasant

distraction, so good, this music of God,
his calming voice. Wonderful odors

everywhere—these dark, human odors.
Sometimes I would taste them. And the salt

of mother's breast, yes, and then that sweet milk
of dreams, dreams and appalling distance.

2. MY PERSONAL HISTORY

Mother bore me without pain.
Something of a miracle I'd say.
Father never doubted my love.
My brother was my better self.
All these frail poems
—beloved sisters.

Good fortune everywhere.
Grace, abundant and wet on our faces.
Exotic fruits plentiful as grass.
God still humming his engaging lyric
in my ear. Air?
Tender, sweet cake.

Just out the door—a jungle.
Just out the door—a blue sea.
And always, between sleep
and waking, between waking
and sleep, this marvelous
confusion of a jungle and a sea.

And later, so many beautiful
women to marry.
They all cared for me.
I married the most generous.

We have a daughter
who resembles me,
but so prettily.
A great miracle.

One morning we three
slept luxuriously in the same bed.

In her drowse, the baby nursed.
God loves Raimundo.
I woke first.

3. MY LANGUAGE

Portuguese is my language,
and that is appropriate.
That is as it should be.

A language somewhat akin
to Spanish, but with ironic
possibilities as well. A perfect
language for my purposes.
One does not weep in Portuguese.

Can you hear its music, its
intelligent distance? (No, of course not.
You are not reading Portuguese now.)

The boats in the harbor are rapt
in conversation with the sea.
The air sings high Portuguese.

When I was a boy, I nearly learned
German too. A narrow escape.
I am careful to avoid things German,
in particular the food. As for English,
I leave that now to whomever needs it.
I never look north from Florianopolis.

Here, I have everything I need: a generous woman,
this daughter, my garden, Portuguese.

4. MY MORTAL DREAM

In which I am driving through what I presume
to be a northamerican city: I have never seen
a northamerican city, but I think this one is St. Louis.
It is not a very clean city, even the air has fingerprints,
windows of the huge tenements are without glass.
The few people I catch sight of are sleepwalking.

At the signal I stop my car, which I believe
is a Volkswagen. I wait for the light and examine
my surroundings. A man with a gun is taking money
from a station attendant. He counts the bills
and shoots the man, who then seems a boy, and now
a sack of leaves. The criminal lifts his face to mine
and I nod. He points. I turn to face the light. The car
window explodes in my ear, and my life begins.

5. MY IMITATION

I sold my possessions, even the colorful pencils.
I gave all my money to the dull. I gave my poverty
to the president. I became a child again, naked
and relatively innocent. I let the president have my guilt.

I found a virgin and asked her to be my mother.
She held me very sweetly.

I watched father build beautiful shapes with wood.
He too had a gentle way.

I made conversation in holy places with the chosen.
Their theater was grim.

I suggested they cheer up. Many repented,
albeit elaborately.

I floated the wide river on a raft.
I set Jim free.

I revised every word.

One morning, very early, I was taken by brutes and beaten.
I was nailed to a cross so sturdy I thought
father himself might have shaped it.

I gestured for a cool drink and was mocked.
I took on the sins of the world and regretted my extravagance.
I gave up and died. I descended into hell
and spoke briefly with the president.

I rose again, bloodless and feeling pretty good.

I forgave everything.

6. OUR LOST ANGELS

Ages ago, clouds brought them near
      and rain brought them to our lips;
      they swam in every vase, every cupped palm.
      We took them into ourselves
      and were refreshed.
For those luckier generations, angels
      were the sweet, quickening substance
      in all light, all water, every morsel of food.
Until the day the sun changed some, as it had,
      took them skyward, but thereafter
      the clouds failed to restore them.
In time, streams gave up
      every spirit, and the sea, unreplenished,
      finally became the void we had feared
      it would become, the void we had imagined.
And, as now, clouds brought only rain,
      and the emptied rain
      brought only the chill in which
      we must now be wrapped.

7. EMBARRASSMENT

The witness caught Raimundo's drift and looked away.
A stale taste dried his open mouth.

The girl in the upper room dressed the ancient doll.
The witness spat, began to pout.

Raimundo shrugs and scribbles on a yellow pad.
The problem's not so simple. Stick around.

8. MY GOODNESS

I have such good intentions.
I have enormous sympathy.
I am aware of a number
of obligations.

In the Hebrew, Enoch
walked with God and was no more.
A difficult translation,
but so intriguing!

I am a little skeptical,
but nonetheless intrigued.
How far must one walk
in such cases?

I suppose I shouldn't tell you,
but I have suspected something
like this. I have had an inkling.
Call it a hunch.

Even so, I manage so little faith.
My goodness is deficient.
I walk for days and looking up
bump again into my own door.

9. MY INCREDULITY

Lazarus, of course,
is another story altogether.

Lazarus does not
engage my better self, nor interest me.

Drink twice from the same
wrong cup? Say the idiot boy falls down,

gets back up and falls
again—this is some great trick?

Our giddy crowd should swoon?
Does the first runner turn back to mock the lost?

And if he does, should we
praise him for his extravagant bad taste?

No. His sort will not
profit close attention. His story—

neither lawful nor
expedient. Tear your linens to winding cloth.

Wrap him once for all.
When you've finished with your napkin, bind his lips.

He has had his say.
Bury Lazarus as often as it takes.

Such a very long night. So demanding
of one's better judgement. I was alone.

Or I seemed alone. My friends had all left
on earlier trains. The raised platform

I paced was poorly lit, my train not due
for another hour. Then the strange man came.

He walked past me once, then turned, surprised;
his appearance—either frightened or insane.

He pronounced a name—certainly foreign—
asked if we hadn't perhaps met before.

If he was familiar, it was nothing
more than a resemblance to any chance

acquaintance. I told him no, he was mistaken.
The wind came up like a howl. He left me.

From behind my book I watched him settle in
at the platform's farthest end. I checked the time,

my train still far away. Then, the soldiers came,
maybe a dozen soldiers. They appeared

suddenly and from every passage.
They came to me rudely, demanded my name.

I told them my business. I was waiting
for a train. Their captain pointed to the stranger

at the platform's end and asked me
if I knew the man. No, I said, I am only

waiting for a train. They ignored me and ran
to the other's bench. They slapped him awake,

picked him up by his coatfront and began
dragging him my way. As they pushed past,

I asked what he had done. The captain stopped,
asked why I had to know. Was I his friend?

No, I said, I've never seen him before tonight.
I don't know the man at all. Take him.

II. MY GOOD LUCK

Fortunately, there are mitigating circumstances.
Fortunately, Raimundo doesn't get what he deserves.
Confronted by embarrassment, I lift my bed and walk.

The comfort lies in fingering the incoherent for the true.
The comfort lies in suspecting more than evidence allows.
My only rule: If I understand something, it's no mystery.

As you might suppose, I miss my father very much;
and if I think of his dying, I can become deeply sad.
Giving yourself to appearances can do a lot of harm.

So I remember the morning my father died, and the ache
of his relief, the odd, uncanny joy which began then,
and which returns unbidden, undeserved, mercifully.

12. MY AMUSING DESPAIR

I confess that I am not
a modern man. As a modern man
I am a little flawed.
Raimundo is much too happy.

Many times, more times
than I would care to admit to you,
I have suffered from this
unforgivable lack, this absence.

All around me, poets
tearing at their bright blouses, tearing
at their own bare flesh.
All night long—their tortured singing.

And still I have suffered
an acute lack of despair. Why is that?
Is Raimundo stupid?
Am I unfeeling? Doesn't the bleak

weight of the north ever
pinch my shoulders? Well, no, not often.
And when it does—which is
not very often—I can't help feeling

a little detached. As if
I had somewhere else to go. As if
I were a spectator,
a dayworker watching the slow clock.
I have an interest in the outcome,
but not a strong interest.

13. MY FAREWELL

Things are happening. Daily,
I come across new disturbances
in my routine. I am curiously
unsettled. I dress myself
and the clothes fall to the floor.
I scratch my head. Dust
in my hand. All morning
arranging flowers, and for what?
Petals fallen, litter
on the pretty cloth. I march
straightway to the mirror
and shake my fist. My hand
is a blue maraca scattering petals.
I shout my rage
and hear my words praising
the vast goodness of the world.
This is beyond control.

Even so, I am slowly learning one thing;
of one thing I am slowly becoming
aware: whether or not I would
have it so, whether I sleep
or no, I will be changed.
I am changing as I speak. Bless you all.
Suffer the children. Finished. Keep.

The Contemporary Poetry Series

EDITED BY PAUL ZIMMER

The Contemporary Poetry Series

EDITED BY BIN RAMKE